NATIONAL GEOGRAPHIC

D0100730

Fruit Salad

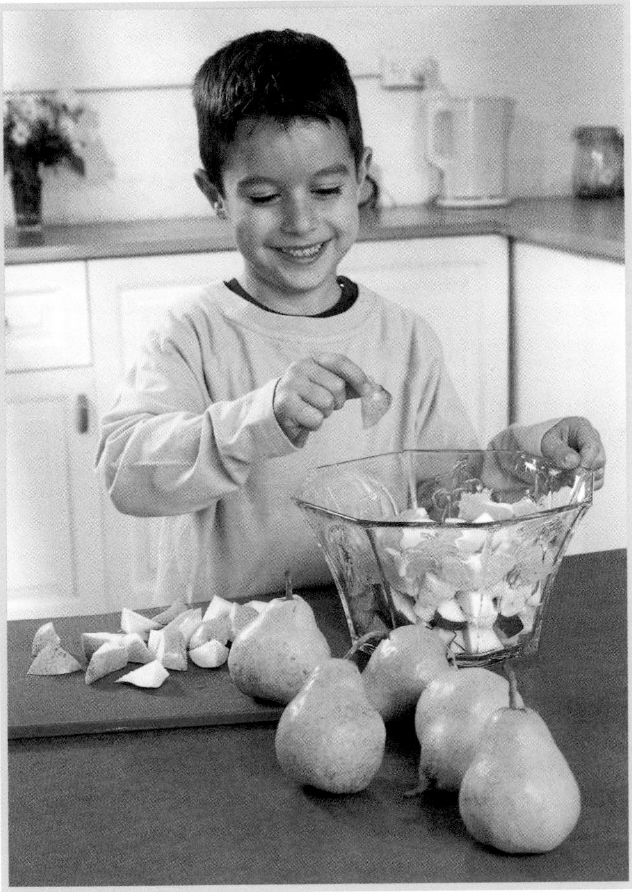

Ming Tan

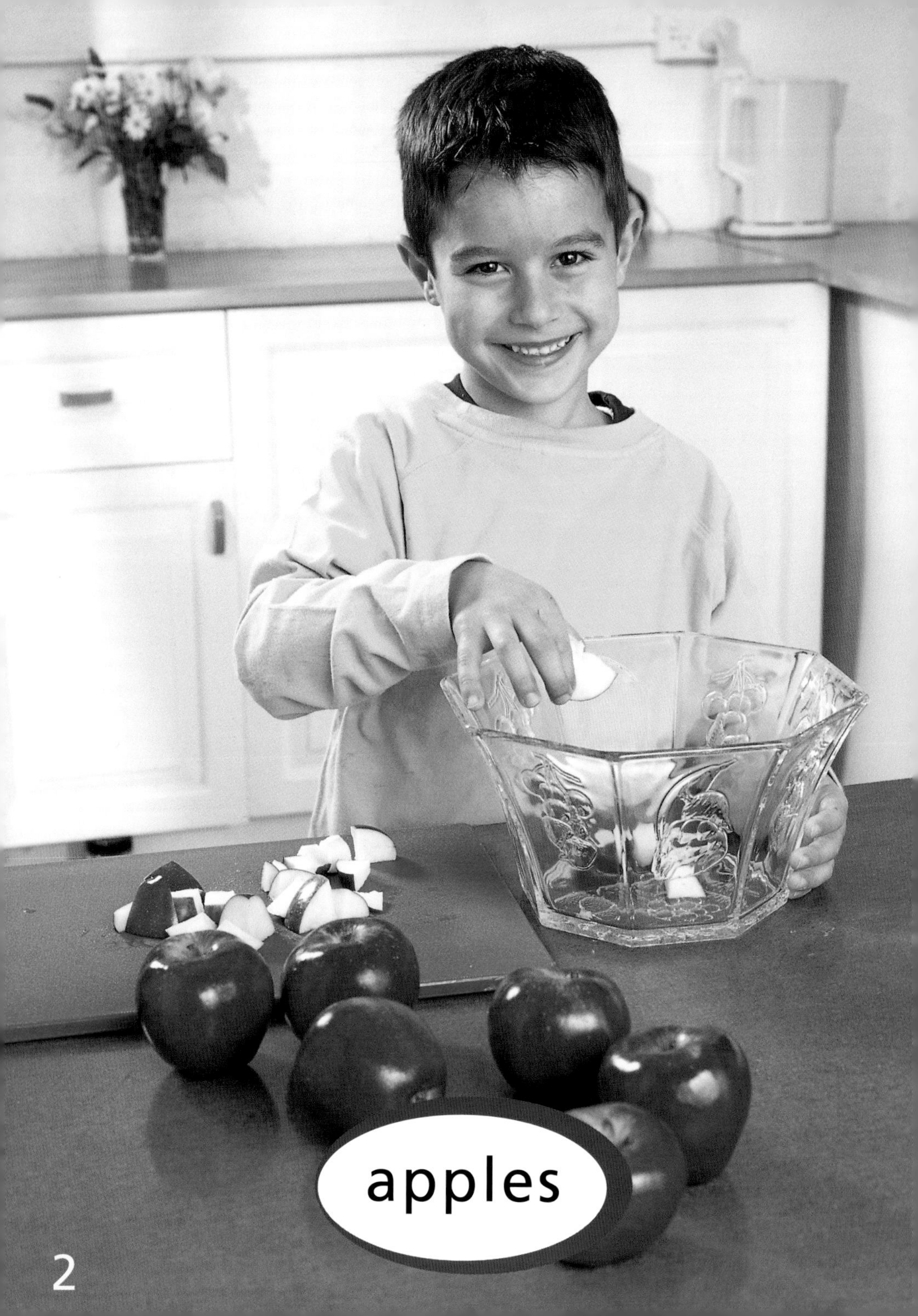

apples

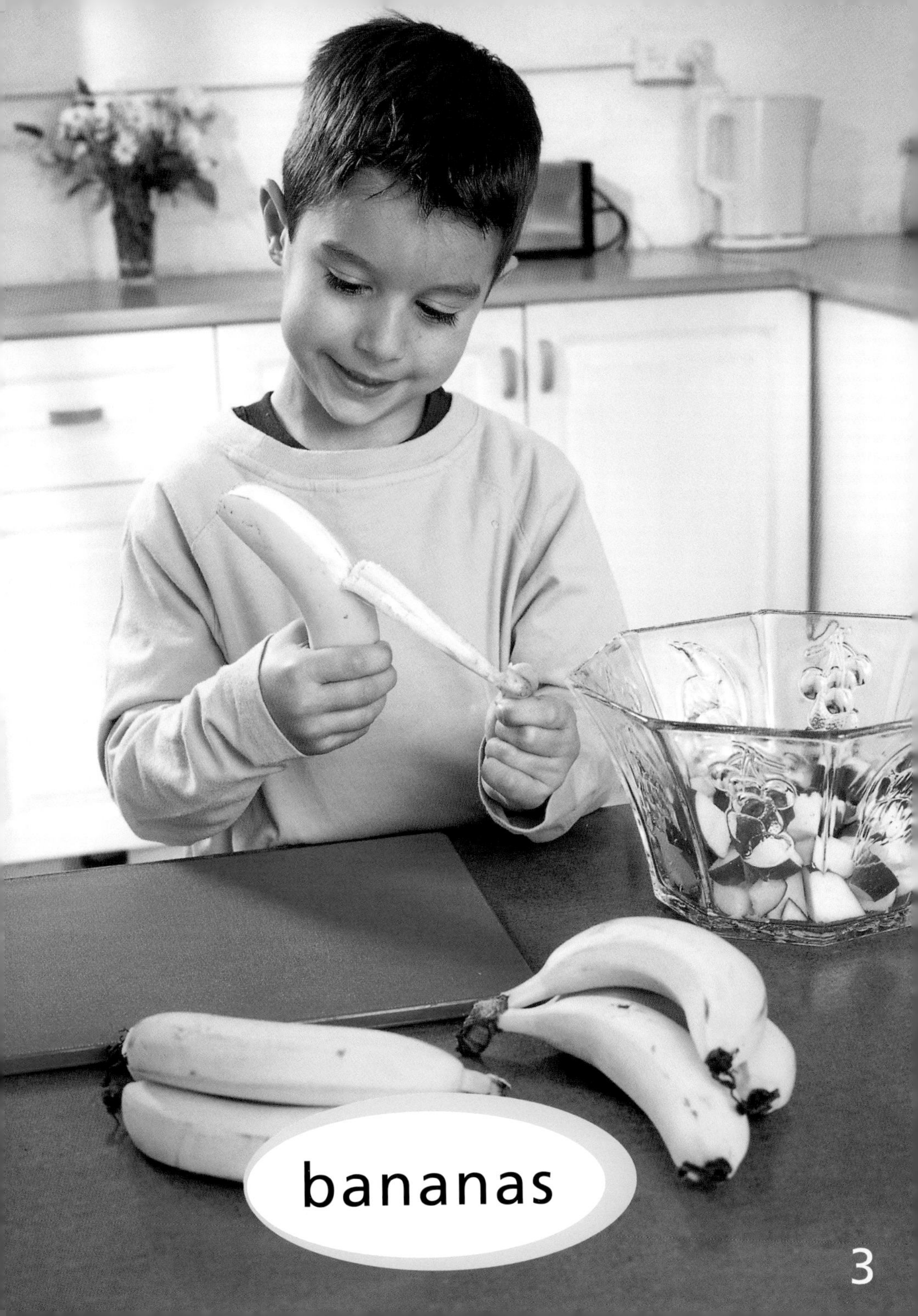

bananas

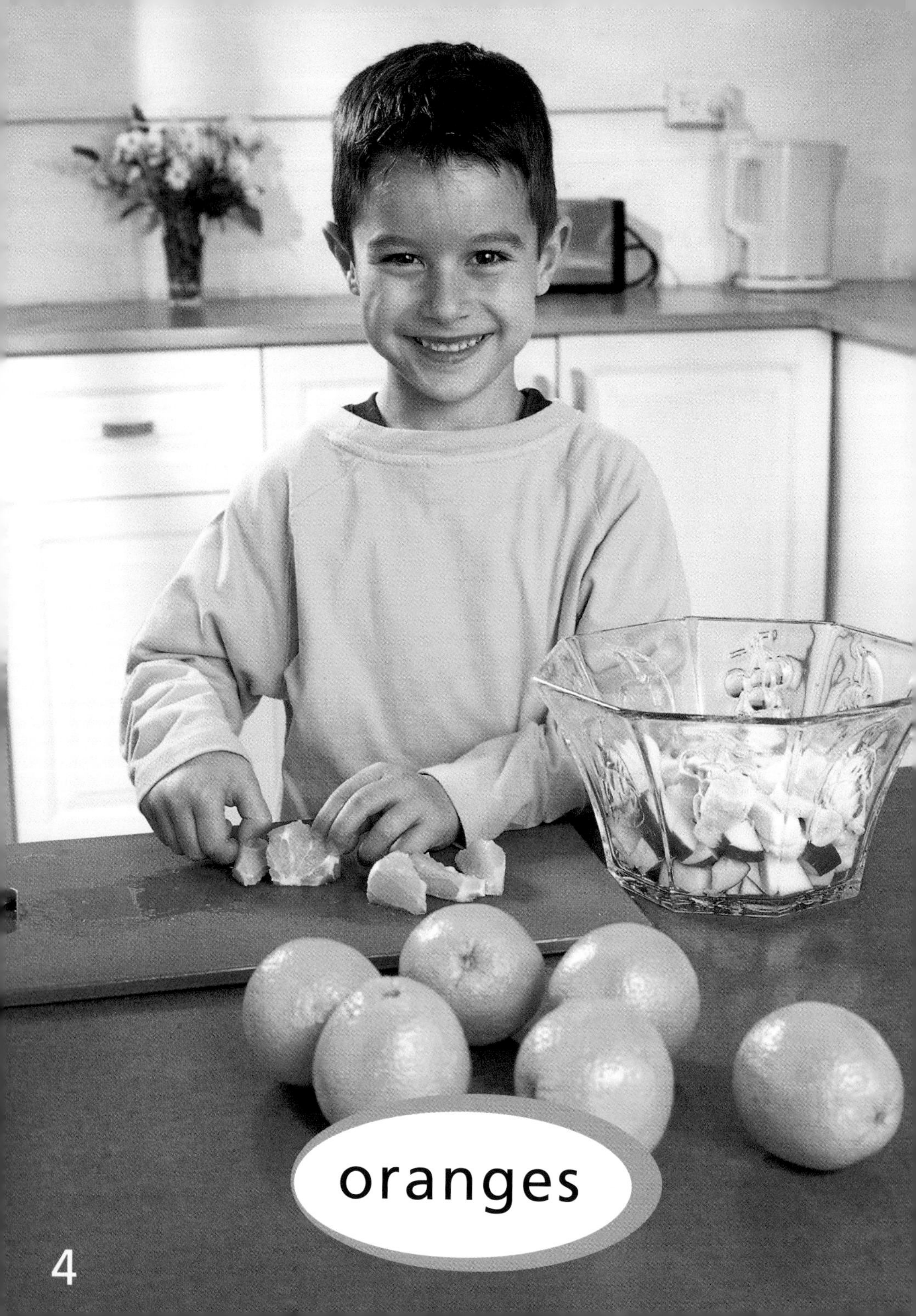

oranges

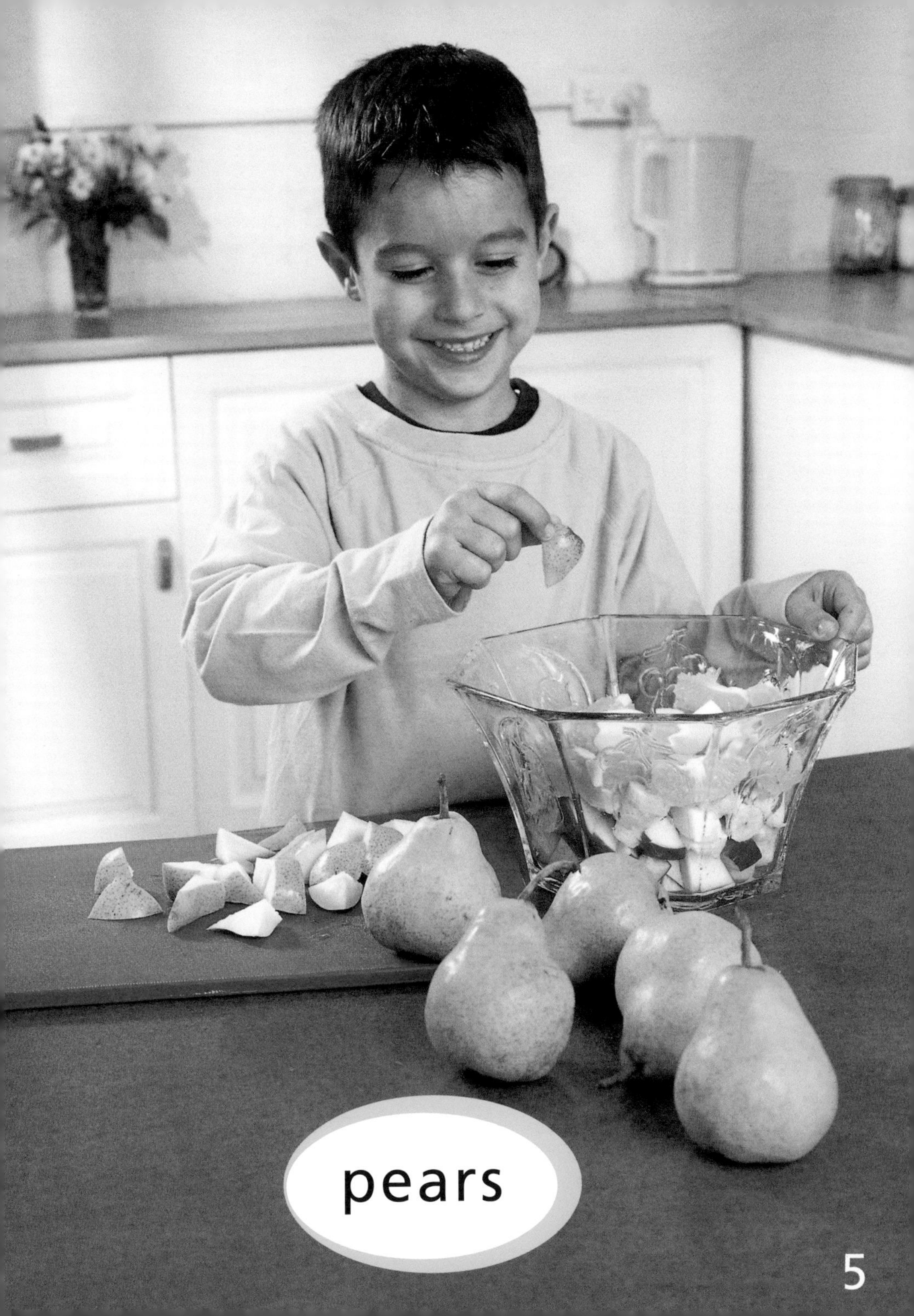

pears

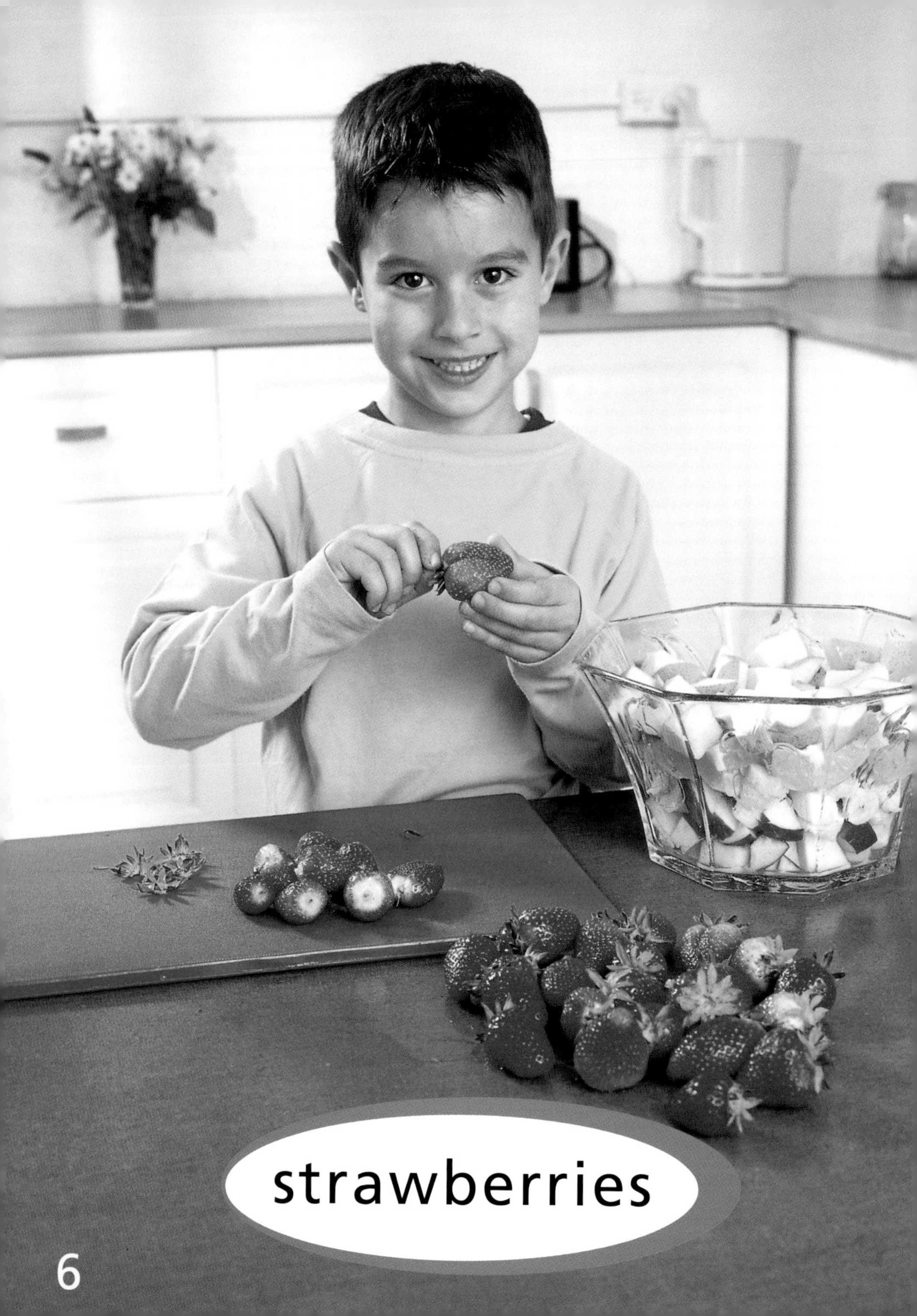

strawberries

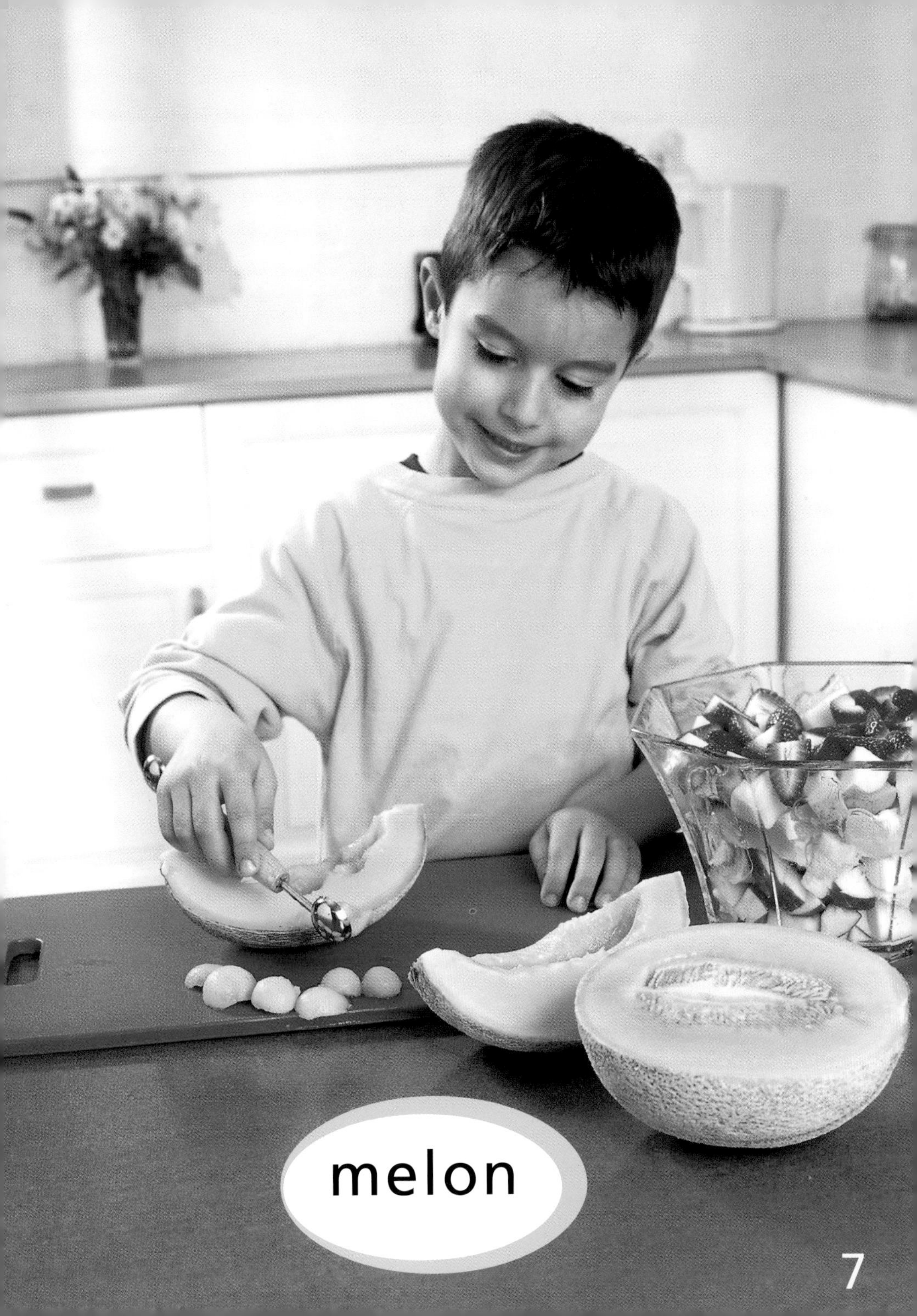

melon

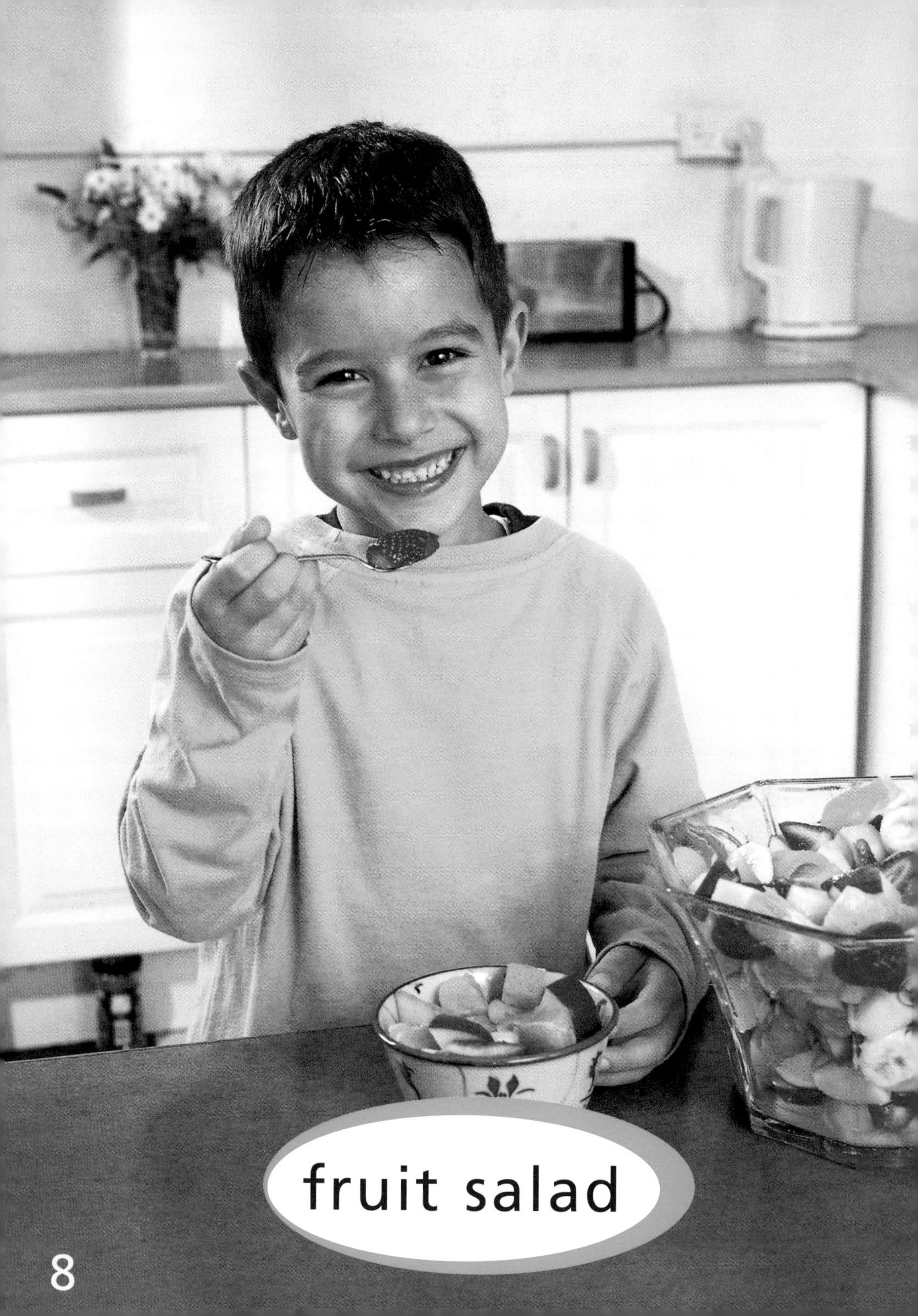

fruit salad